Swayam Ganguly was born in Jamshedpur and currently resides in Kolkata. He wears many hats, being a published author, director of corporate films, and editorial consultant for various publishers. He has worked on biographies, mythology series, abridged versions of classics, encyclopedias, fact books, and also written children's fiction.

Also in the Incredible Life series:

Jhalkari Bai: The Braveheart Warrior

Milkha Singh: The Runner Who Could Fly

Birsa Munda: The Great Revolutionary Leader

Savitribai Phule: The Fearless Reformer

Bhagat Singh: The Indomitable Freedom Fighter

Arati Saha: The Swimmer Who Wouldn't Give Up

Anandibai Joshee: The Girl Who Fought to Be a Doctor

Satyendranath Bose: A Great Scientist of the World

Mary Kom: The Queen of Boxing

The Incredible Life of APJ Abdul Kalam

The Visionary Man of Science

Swayam Ganguly

Illustrations by

talking CUB
An Imprint of Speaking Tiger Books

TALKING CUB

Published by Speaking Tiger Books LLP
125A, Ground Floor, Shahpur Jat,
Near Asiad Village, New Delhi 110 049

First published in paperback in Talking Cub
by Speaking Tiger Books in 2024

ISBN: 978-93-5447-929-8

eISBN: 978-93-5447-806-2

10 9 8 7 6 5 4 3 2 1

Typeset in Georgia by Jojy Philip
Printed at

To my wife, Piali

Chapter One

It was early evening in the island city of Rameswaram. The sun dipped below the horizon to paint the sky with a multicoloured display of luminous reds and yellows. The devotees folded their hands to pay their respects to Lord Rama, who had left the Indian mainland for Sri Lanka by building a bridge from this very place.

Despite that, the Ramanathaswamy Temple, dedicated to Lord Shiva, is the most famous landmark of Rameswaram. A ten-minute walk away, stands an old mosque in a predominantly

Muslim locality, where evening prayers had just concluded. Jainulabdeen walked out, holding his little boy's hand. The meaning of the Arabic prayers chanted in the mosque was incomprehensible to the boy, but he was positive that they reached God. Little did anyone know then that the little boy named Abdul Kalam would, in his life, bring further glory to Rameswaram.

Born on 15 October 1931, Kalam was the youngest son of Jainulabdeen and Ashiamma. Kalam had a humble upbringing. His middle-class Tamil family lived in their nineteenth century ancestral house—a modest structure built of limestone and brick. While his parents shunned nonessential comforts and luxuries, food, medicines, clothes, and education always received top priority in the household. The food

served was simple yet sumptuous. Kalam and his siblings (four brothers and one sister) sat on the floor, cross-legged, during meal-time as their mother served them.

Despite lacking formal education and wealth, Jainulabdeen possessed wisdom, generosity, and kindness. He had a knack for explaining complex spiritual concepts in the simplest of words. 'Every human being,' he would say to Kalam, 'in his own time and own place, in what he really is, and in the good or bad stage he has reached, is a specific element within the whole of the manifest Divine Being.'

He would advise his son not to be afraid of struggles and difficulties, but to take them in his stride. He taught him that adversity always provided room for introspection and betterment.

Kalam's father was his idol, and he tried to emulate his father's ideals and discipline in his own world of science and technology later.

When Kalam was six-years-old, his father built a sailboat with the help of a relative, Ahmed Jallaluddin, to ferry pilgrims from Rameswaram to Dhanuskodi and back. With Jallaluddin spending long hours at Kalam's house, a new friendship was born between the man and the young boy. Although fifteen years apart, the duo became the closest of friends. They would go for long walks in the evening, their first stop being the majestic temple of Lord Shiva. Jallaluddin, who fondly called Kalam 'Azad', would speak about the importance of education, medical discoveries, scientific achievements, and contemporary literature to fuel ambition in Kalam, who learnt of the brave, big world that existed outside the narrow confines of Rameswaram.

In 1939, as India joined the British and the Allied forces to fight the Axis powers in the Second World War, a state of Emergency was declared in the entire country. Earlier, the morning train from Pamban delivered the newspapers to the small Rameswaram station early in the morning. With the Emergency declared, trains no longer stopped at Rameswaram, and the newspaper had to be thrown out of the moving trains. However, this seeminglydarkcloud had a silver lining. Samsuddin, the sole distributor of newspapers in

the town, realised he needed someone young and fit to catch the flying bundles. And who else would be better for the job than his young cousin, Abdul Kalam? Samsuddin hired Kalam to be his newspaper boy and Kalam, at the young age of eight discovered a sense of pride in earning his own money. It was a win-win situation!

1939 witnessed many remarkable events that shaped the course of history and popular culture:

- January 6: A Jewish woman, Lise Meitner from Vienna published her discovery—'atom splitting'—during her exile in Sweden.
- January 16: The daily newspaper comic strip 'Superman' made its debut.
- January 20: Adolf Hitler declared his plan to exterminate all European Jews to the parliament.

- March 3: Mahatma Gandhi began a fast in Bombay, in protest against British autocratic rule in India.
- May 3: Subhas Chandra Bose announced the formation of the All India Forward Bloc.
- August 2: Albert Einstein corresponded with President Franklin Roosevelt about using Uranium to develop the atomic bomb.

Hindus and Muslims lived peacefully together in Rameswaram. Kalam's father was a close friend of Pakshi Lakshmana Sastry, the high priest of the Ramanathaswamy Temple and Kalam's best friend in Rameswaram Elementary School was Ramanadha Sastry, the high priest's son. With such a secular surrounding, Kalam grew up listening to bedtimes stories about episodes from the Ramayana and tales about the life of the Prophet.

However, an unfortunate incident during the fifth standard, shattered all this. A new teacher had started teaching, and he did not like that a Muslim boy was sitting next to the son of a Hindu priest. Kalam was asked to shift to the back of the class. Although later the teacher was rebuked by Lakshmana Sastry and he reformed his regressive ways, the image of Ramanadha weeping at the separation from his friend left

a lasting impression on Kalam's mind. But not all teachers in Rameswaram were so orthodox in their beliefs. Kalam's science teacher, Sivasubramania Iyer—despite hailing from an orthodox Brahmin family—was a rebel, hell-bent on breaking all regressive social barriers. Once, he had invited Kalam to his house for a meal. When his horrified wife refused to serve a Muslim boy, Iyer lovingly served the boy himself and even ate with him.

By and by, the Second World War concluded; India's freedom too from the long British rule was imminent now. With the prospect of a new India beckoning, fifteen-year-old Abdul Kalam travelled to Ramananthapuram to enrol in Schwartz High School in 1945.

Chapter Two

Kalam completed his education at Schwartz, and got admission in St Joseph's College, Tiruchirappalli, in 1950. There he spent four years. When Kalam was introduced to the concepts of physics, the young man fell deeply in love with the subject. He was fascinated by the movement of electrons around each nucleus in each object of the Universe—'It was as if Lord Shiva was performing his great cosmic dance during each moment of our existence,' he thought.

Even as a child, Kalam was fascinated by the world around him, constantly asking questions about how things worked. He would spend hours watching birds fly, wondering what made them soar through the air with such ease.

'I want to fly like the bird one day!' he thought.

But, it was only after he had completed his Bachelors in Science (BSc.) that Kalam realised that despite his love for physics, only that wouldn't help him fly like birds. Instead, he had to study engineering. So, he applied to Madras Institute of Technology (MIT), the premier institute of technical education in South India at the time.

Kalam had always been a bright and hardworking student, so he easily cleared the admission test. The problem that arose instead was money. Education at a prestigious institution was expensive—a thousand rupees was required for admission, which poor Jainulabdeen, with his meagre earnings, couldn't afford. Kalam felt his wings being clipped even before he took flight! It was his sister Zohara who came to Kalam's rescue, rustling up the money by mortgaging her gold jewellery. Kalam was deeply moved.

'I shall release Zohara's jewellery from mortgage with my first earnings!' he vowed.

Two decommissioned aircrafts were on display at the MIT campus. Seeing those massive metal birds, Kalam could almost see his childhood dream right in front of his eyes. So, with his first year at MIT done and dusted, he chose aeronautical engineering for his specialisation without a second thought.

'I am going to fly an aircraft!' Kalam thought.

Aeronautical engineering is a subfield of aerospace engineering. It focuses on the designing, development, testing, and the production of aircrafts.

Aeronautical engineering refers to the navigation of an aircraft within the earth's atmosphere while aerospace engineering is the study involving navigation outside the earth's atmosphere.

The study of aeronautical engineering is all about the designing and development of atmospheric vehicles like planes, helicopters, and unmanned aerial vehicles like drones. In comparison, aerospace engineers design, develop, and maintain space vehicles like rockets and spacecraft.

Kalam was surrounded by superstars of aeronautical engineering, each a specialist in fields like aero-structure design, theoretical aerodynamics and technical aerodynamics. Once Kalam was assigned a project to design a low-level attack aircraft along with four other colleagues at MIT. Professor Srinivasan, the Director of MIT, was the design teacher heading the project. He informed Kalam that the project was progressing at a slow pace and needed to be completed faster.

Kalam requested for a month to complete the task.

'I'll give you three days,' Prof. Srinivasan declared. 'If I don't get the configuration drawing by Monday, your scholarship will be revoked.'

Thunderstruck, young Kalam felt utterly helpless. He wouldn't be able to achieve anything without MIT's generous scholarship. Determined to never let that happen, he immersed himself at work, even skipping dinner on Friday night. On Saturday morning, he took only an hour's break to freshen up and eat some food. He had almost completed his drawing on Sunday morning when Prof. Srinivasan entered the room.

The old director hugged Kalam lovingly and patted his back in appreciation after examining the work. 'I knew I was setting an impossible

deadline for you,' he stated. 'I never expected you to meet it, and perform so well.'

The years at MIT passed in a blur. Soon it was time for graduation. On the day of graduation, during the farewell photograph with the graduating students and the professors, Professor Sponder, who taught technical aerodynamics, sought Kalam and asked him to sit with him in the front. As an emotional Kalam moved from the third row to the front of the group, the professor proudly declared, 'You are my best student, and I am sure your hard work will make us teachers proud in the future.'

With a post-graduation from MIT in his bag, Kalam joined Hindustan Aeronautics Limited (HAL), Bangalore as a trainee, working on engine overhauling of piston and turbine engines. The practical experience served him well to master concepts of gas dynamics and the working dynamics of propeller engines.

At HAL, the people Kalam learnt from did not have university degrees, but their hands-on-experience, acquired over the years, taught Kalam valuable lessons. When he finally graduated as a successful aeronautical engineer, a determined Kalam applied for jobs both at the Air Force and at the Directorate of Technical Development and Production, DTD&P (Air) at the Ministry of Defence. With his experience and expertise, the interview calls arrived simultaneously for both positions and he was summoned to Dehradun by the Air Force and to Delhi by DTD&P (Air).

For the first time in his young life, Abdul Kalam left his native south and boarded a train to travel the long distance of over 2000 km.

Chapter Three

Kalam reached Delhi. His interview with DTD&P (Air) went well, and he travelled to Dehradun next for his interview with the Air Force Selection Board. After a rigorous selection, Kalam finished ninth in the batch of twenty-five candidates interviewed. However, only eight officers were to be selected for the IAF.

Dejected to have missed out so narrowly, Kalam trekked to Rishikesh to calm his mind. He bathed in the holy Ganga and walked to the Sivananda Ashram, seeking answers to the doubts that plagued his mind.

At the ashram, he had the chance to meet the gracious sage with a childlike smile, Swami Sivananda. Many had often said that the sage resembled the Buddha.

'What is your name, young man?'

When Kalam introduced himself, his Muslim name did not evoke any reaction in the Swamiji.

'What is the cause of your sorrow?' he asked.

Kalam told him about his long-cherished dream to fly and the unsuccessful attempt to join the Indian Air Force.

Swami Sivananda listened to Kalam patiently. Then, he told Kalam to accept his destiny and carry on with his life.

'You are not destined to be an Air Force pilot,'

he said. 'Whatever you are destined to be is predetermined.

'Search for the true purpose of your existence,' Swamiji advised. 'Surrender to God's wish!'

This meeting jolted Kalam. On returning to Delhi, he went straight to the DTD&P (Air), inquiring about the result of his interview. He was handed his appointment letter in response.

At the age of twenty-seven, Abdul Kalam joined the DTD&P (Air) as Senior Scientific Assistant on a monthly salary of Rs 250. This was the beginning of a glorious journey he would take as a man of science in India!

The year was 1958. Kalam was posted at the Technical Centre (Civil Aviation). Although he wasn't flying airplanes, he was helping build them. Much like everywhere else,

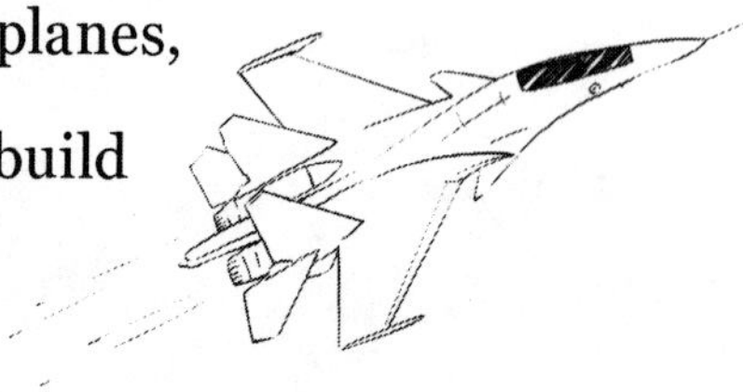

he excelled in his job, even completing a design of a supersonic target aircraft, which earned him praise from the Director.

As appreciation for his skills, Kalam was sent to the Aircraft and Armament Testing Unit at Kanpur to learn more about aircraft maintenance and on returning to Delhi, he joined the design team. Over his years in the team, he completed a variety of designs—a DART target and a Vertical Takeoff and Landing Platform with his team members. His crowning glory was however, the construction and development of the Hot Cockpit. After three years at the DTD&P,

Kalam was posted to the new establishment in Bangalore called the Aeronautical Development Establishment (ADE).

Bangalore was a sharp contrast to Kanpur. It was a city with many scientific establishments and a laidback, pleasant climate. The workload at the ADE was light initially, and Kalam took to exploring the gardens of Bangalore in the evenings. But his breezy life soon became hectic when Kalam was included on a small project team to design an indigenous hovercraft prototype as a ground equipment machine (GEM).

Kalam was asked to lead the team and was given three years to launch the engineering model. This project was much bigger than the collective abilities of the team, none of whom had the experience of building a machine, let alone

one that flew. There were no reference designs or standard components available to create a heavier-than-air flying machine. But taking the challenge in his stride, Kalam decided to go ahead with whatever was available. 'Hadn't the Wright Brothers made the first aeroplane after fixing bicycles for seven long years!' he thought.

Everyone the ADE called Kalam and his team eccentric inventors chasing an impossible dream. Being the leader, Kalam was especially the target of frequent taunts. But none of this deterred them from the project.

When the project was a year old, Defence Minister Krishna Menon visited the ADE to check the progress. He fired questions like bullets at Kalam, determined that the prototype would go into test flight by the next year.

The first practical hovercraft was developed by the English engineer, Sir Cristopher Cockerell. The SR.N1 made its maiden voyage in 1959.

Hovercrafts are innovative vehicles operating on a cushion of air to hover just above the surface to traverse diverse landscapes like land, water, and ice, among others.

Hovercrafts have been used for civilian and military purposes like transportation and rescue missions.

The Russian-made Zubr-class was the largest hovercraft in the world and could carry heavy loads like tanks and troops.

The use of hovercraft technology has inspired futuristic urban transportation designs like high-speed trains.

The hovercraft was named Nandi, after Lord Shiva's bull. 'Here's a flying machine not made by a bunch of cranks, but constructed by engineers of ability,' Kalam addressed his sceptical colleagues. 'Don't look at it, as it is not made to look at, but to fly.'

With Kalam at the helm, the Defence Minister took his maiden flight in Nandi. Although an experienced Group Captain in the minister's troupe was worried about Menon's safety and offered to fly the prototype himself, Kalam refused. It was *his* machine and *he* knew who would best fly it!

Instead of being offended, Defence Minister Menon was impressed by Kalam's determination. Suffice to say, he had a very enjoyable ride.

'Go for a more powerful prime mover, and call me for another ride!' he declared.

Kalam's team finished the project ahead of schedule. Nandi was a working hovercraft now, capable of moving substantial weight above the ground. Sadly, Krishna Menon could not take the second ride. With him out of office and the new order reluctant to spend money on indigenous military hovercrafts, the project was shelved.

Kalam, who had put his heart and soul into Nandi, felt truly disappointed and disillusioned.

But all was not lost. Soon after, Director Dr Mediratta asked Kalam to organise a demonstration for an important visitor. The tall, handsome, and bearded man took a ten-minute ride with Kalam on Nandi after asking him several questions on the hovercraft. Then he left, without saying anything.

Confused, Kalam didn't know what to make of this interaction. Then something miraculous happened!

A week later, Kalam received a call from the Indian Committee for Space Research (INCOSPAR). He had been called for an interview for the post of Rocket Engineer. Along with the other researchers, there was that same tall, handsome, bearded man, taking Kalam's interview!

The next evening, to his utter elation, Kalam was informed that he was selected as a rocket engineer at INCOSPAR.

Modern rocket-based research was finally emerging in India and INCOSPAR was taking the lead. The innovative inventions began with the Equatorial Rocket Launching Station at Thumba in Kerala in 1962. Kalam was a part of it all—he was even sent to the US for a six-month training programme on sounding rocket launching techniques at NASA. The young man was steadily moving towards his childhood dream and nothing could stop him!

Before leaving for the US, Kalam visited Rameswaram. The small town was elated to see their young Kalam reaching such tall heights.

Jainulabdeen organised a special namaz in thanksgiving at the mosque. Jallaluddin and Samsuddin came to see Kalam off at Bombay airport. They were emotional, and in tears.

'Azad, we love you, and believe in you!' Jallaluddin declared. 'We shall always be proud of you!'

Chapter Four

United States of America, 1963! Thirty-two-year-old Abdul Kalam reached the Langley Research Centre in Virginia. From scholars and engineers there, Kalam learnt all that he could about rockets for the next six months. He also visited NASA's premier centres—the Goddard Space Flight Centre in Maryland and the Wallops Flight Facility in Virginia.

At the Wallops reception lobby, Kalam was surprised to see a painting of a battle scene with rockets flying in the background. Intrigued, he observed the painting carefully and to his fascination, realised that the soldiers were from Tipu Sultan's army fighting the British. What an honour it was to see his country man being glorified as a warfare rocketry hero by none other than NASA!

TIPU SULTAN: THE FATHER OF WAR ROCKETS

Tipu Sultan's army manufactured rockets called Mysorean or Tipu rockets. The rockets were made of metal tubes filled with gunpowder, and had stabilising rods at the rear.

Tipu's army was divided into twenty-seven brigades called Kushoons, and each brigade had a company of rocket men called Jourks. The rocket corps had over 5000 trained men, who had mastered the launch and elevation of their weapon to hit precise targets.

The British were unaware of this war technology, and were afraid of these Mysorean rockets that caused havoc on the battlefield.

When Tipu Sultan was eventually defeated and killed, the British captured over 700 rockets and subsystems of 900 rockets in 1799. These rockets were taken to England, and subjected to what we term 'reverse engineering' today.

India's first rocket launch took place on 21 November 1963, soon after Kalam's return from the USA. The sounding rocket was called Nike-Apache and was made at NASA. Kalam was put in charge and the launch was successful.

India's scientists and engineers were jubilant at seeing her strive towards the stars.

The successful rocket launch seemed to fuel inspiration in the hearts of all Indians. Soon, the rocket launch site at the sleepy fishing village in Kerala was developed into the Thumba Equatorial Rocket Launch Station (TERLS), with collaborations with the USSR, USA, and France.

The goal was to create a national space programme to manufacture and develop rockets within the country. The Rohini Sounding Rocket (RSR) Programme was the first to successfully achieve this goal. The RSR led to the development and creation of a family of sounding rockets with wide-ranging capabilities for scientific and technological studies.

Indian rocketry was reborn after the eighteenth century thanks to Prime Minister Jawaharlal Nehru's vision and Dr Vikram Sarabhai's efforts. They believed that if India wanted to have a strong voice in the world, it needed to rely on its own ingenuity and build advanced technologies. Their goal wasn't to show off military power, but to develop rockets and satellites that could help solve real-life problems faced by everyday Indians.

Under Dr Sarabhai's able leadership, Kalam and his team members made indigenous rockets, satellites, and satellite launch vehicles. Kalam was assigned the responsibility to provide interface support to payload scientists. These payloads needed to be integrated into the rocket structure for proper functioning and endurance during flight.

One day, Kalam and his colleague Sudhakar were handling a volatile mixture of sodium and thermite. These were usually used to fuel rockets and could turn deadly in a heartbeat. The duo worked meticulously, their each movement calculated and precious. Suddenly, a drop of sweat from Sudhakar's forehead fell onto the sodium. A violent explosion ripped through the payload room, engulfing it in flames. Kalam froze, fear paralysing him. Water, which usually extinguished fire would only make the sodium fire worse.

It was Sudhakar who turned out to be the hero that day! Displaying great presence of mind, he broke the glass window using his bare hands, shoved Kalam towards safety first, and then jumped out himself. Even through the searing pain, Sudhakar managed a faint smile as Kalam grasped his bleeding hands in gratitude. He had saved a friend, but the cost was high. Sudhakar spent several weeks in the hospital recovering from severe burns.

In February 1969, Prime Minister Indira Gandhi visited Thumba to dedicate TERLS to the International Space Science Community. Slowly and steadily, two Indian rockets, Rohini and Menaka, were born at Thumba, named after celestial dancers at the court of Indra, the king of the Devas. Finally, the Indian payloads did not need to be launched by French rockets anymore.

On 20 November 1967, the first Rohini-75 rocket was launched from TERLS.

In early 1968, Dr Sarabhai urgently summoned Kalam to Delhi. An appointment at 3.30 a.m. was set up at the Hotel Ashoka. As a nervous Kalam waited in the hotel lounge, he noticed a well-built man seated on the sofa opposite him. The gentleman had an aura of intelligence about him. He was wearing smart clothes and appeared alert despite the late hour.

When Kalam was ushered into Dr Sarabhai's room, the stranger went with him.

'Who was this man...' Kalam wondered, 'and why such a secret late-night meeting?'

Dr Sarabhai introduced the man as Group Captain V.S. Narayanan from the Air Headquarters. Through the meeting, he informed the two gentlemen that he wanted them to collaborate to form a Missile Panel in the Ministry of Defence. Both Kalam and Narayanan were inducted as members.

The bitter lessons of the 1962 and 1965 wars had made the Indian leadership determined to be self-reliant. Developing indigenous missiles was therefore the foremost approach of the country's leaders. It was during this time that a large number of Surface to-Air Missiles had been obtained from the USSR. Narayanan advocated they develop these missiles at home.

Kalam and Narayanan made a great team. Narayanan was keen to learn about rocket engineering and Kalam wanted to know more about airborne weapons systems. Thus, the two played the roles of teacher and student interchangeably.

Unfortunately, India still had a long way to go to be truly self-sufficient. Defence Research and Development still heavily depended on imports.

The Missile Project drew up a long shopping list and import plan. Kalam was unhappy. 'Is my nation doomed to work with screwdriver technology?' he wondered.

Practically skipping with excitement, one day, Kalam's young colleague Jaya Chandra Babu, informed him that creating Rocket Assisted Take Off (RATO) systems was possible without imports.

'But there is a roadblock...' he cautioned, his excitement dimming slightly.

If only they could bypass the organisation's sluggish, bureaucratic processes, this would be a game-changer! They needed to shake things up, and the only way to do it was by radicalising their approach and creating a workable system that relied on a smaller, efficient group and took help from the private sector to fast-forward things.

Such bold demands were unheard of in conservative government establishments. Some might have even called them outrageous. But, as Kalam examined Babu's request, he could not help but think that the logic was undeniable. He took the proposal to Dr Sarabhai, who, to his delight, instantly approved them.

Although Babu soon left India for other opportunities in Nigeria, his brief but impactful tenure left behind a crucial lesson: even rocket science could benefit from a dose of business acumen.

Kalam's team crafted a composite structure for the RATO motor casing using light-weight, strong fibre glass and a cutting-edge ignition system. A cleverly angled nozzle deflected the jet fuels away from the aircraft, to keep it safe. A year of tireless experimenting later, the first static test of RATO was conducted. Within the next four months, the small but reliant team of twenty engineers conducted sixty-four static tests.

THE CUBAN MISSILE CRISIS

In October 1962, the world came closest to a nuclear war when the two superpowers, the United States and the Soviet Union were involved in a deadly confrontation during the Cold War.

When the Soviet Union built secret nuclear missile sites on Cuba, President Kennedy blockaded Cuba with a ring of ships around the island to prevent the Soviets from bringing in more military supplies. Kennedy demanded the removal and destruction of the missile sites from Cuba.

It was uncertain how Soviet leader Nikita Khrushchev would react to these demands. Thankfully, both leaders realised the deadly consequences of a nuclear war. Khrushchev ordered the missiles to be dismantled, and Kennedy disbanded American missile sites in Turkey, and pledged not to attack Cuba. The Cuban missile crisis thus ended, after causing a significant scare.

Chapter Five

There were immense benefits of having a space technology in one's own country and Dr Sarabhai knew it. In 1969, he decided to go full-steam ahead to build and launch India's own satellites. He selected the crescent-shaped Sriharikota Island, 100 km north of Madras (now Chennai) as a site to launch satellites and large rockets. Thus, the SHAR Rocket Launch station was born.

In 1968, the Indian Space Research Organisation (ISRO) was formed under the

Department of Atomic Energy. Dr Sarabhai hand-picked a team to create an Indian satellite. Kalam was chosen as a project leader for an important part of the satellite called the Stage 4.

To advise with the design and ideation, Dr Sarabhai took the help of Professor Curien, who was President of CNES (Centre Nationale de Etudes Spatiales), ISRO's counterpart in France. With the French developing similar launch vehicles (Diamont), Prof. Curien's help was a boon to the project.

Although impressed with Kalam and team's work, Prof. Curien wanted to test their abilities. 'I want you to make the fourth stage but using French designs,' the Frenchman instructed one day.

Never shying away from invention, Kalam

was ready for the job. However, the challenge was that the diameters of the French and the Indian satellites were different. So, calculations were becoming tricky.

But Kalam was not one to give up. He decided to innovate and come up with a separate and authentic design. It was such a success that Prof. Curien declared that the Indian team had accomplished in one year what their European counterparts had barely managed in three years!

It took Kalam and his team two years to modify their existing Indian designs to suit the French Diamont framework. They successfully upgraded it from a smaller, lighter stage to a larger, more powerful one. But something unexpected happened after that. When it was due to be delivered to CNES, the French suddenly cancelled their project. This was a great shock but Kalam tried to console himself:

'There will be other projects. I must not dwell on the disappointment for too long and look towards the future.'

Sure enough, the RATO project began, and Kalam forgot about his disappointment. The satellite was simultaneously taking shape.

That year, Dr Sarabhai visited Thumba to see the demonstration of a new rocket system.

Everything was ready and Dr Sarabhai was to activate the machine through a timer. All he had to do was press a button. But, nothing happened when the button was pressed.

Kalam and his team were stunned, this was not supposed to happen. In the end, they decided to remove the timer and give the machine a direct connection.

Dr Sarabhai pressed the button again, and this time everything worked perfectly. But, although he congratulated the team, Kalam could see that the old man's thoughts were elsewhere.

That night, Kalam and Dr Sarabhai had an important discussion.

'Is something on your mind?' asked the older man. 'Are you and your team affected by something that I am not aware of?'

But before Kalam could respond, he seemed to have found the answer himself.

'We need a single space to test all our rocket systems together. Working separately on the mechanical and electrical parts is not doing us any good.'

That day, at the wee hours of the morning, Kalam and Dr Sarabhai decided to form a Rocket Engineering Sector.

Kalam realised that only a visionary like Dr Sarabhai could use errors and mistakes to innovate and develop new ideas. He leant that crisis should always be handled without putting blame on others, and the only way to prevent errors was to predict them before they happened.

Kalam would update Dr Sarabhai after every Missile Panel Meeting. On 30 December 1971, after attending a meeting in Delhi, he called up Dr Sarabhai but was asked to wait at Trivandrum Airport to meet the senior scientist.

Gloom hung in the air when Kalam reached Trivandrum.

'Professor Sarabhai is no more!' Kutty, who worked at the airport, informed in a choked voice. Dr Sarabhai had died of cardiac arrest a few hours ago.

Kalam was shocked. Not only had he lost a mentor and a friend but India had lost a great scientist.

A short time after Dr Sarabhai's passing, with Professor MGK Menon in charge, Professor Satish Dhawan was appointed the head of ISRO. The complex of Thumba, including all its research facilities, were merged to form a single space centre, the Vikram Sarabhai Space Centre (VSSC), in honour of the great man.

On 8 October, 1972, the RATO system was finally successfully tested at the Bareilly Air Force station in Uttar Pradesh. It helped a high-performing jet aircraft to take off using only a short runway of 1200 metres instead of its usual 2 km.

This was a significant achievement. Not only did it save India a lot of money in foreign exchange, the Indian RATO was far cheaper to produce.

Meanwhile, at the VSSC, work on the satellite was on at full swing. But, they were lacking a proper manager who would be able to handle such a big project and coordinate with all the team. Who could be better for the job than Abdul Kalam?

Space launch vehicles mostly trace their origins to ballistic missiles developed for military use during the 1950s and early '60s.

The Sputnik 1 spacecraft was the first artificial satellite successfully placed in orbit around the Earth and was launched by the former Soviet Union.

The two types of launch vehicles are expendable launch vehicles and reusable launch vehicles. Expendable launch vehicles are designed for one-time use only. They have boosters that separate from their payload and disintegrate during atmospheric reentry or ground contact. Reusable launch vehicles are designed to be recovered and launched again.

Satellites do important work in space, and without them, using our cell phones and watching our favourite TV shows would be impossible.

They also help with weather forecast, defence, navigation with Global Positioning System (GPS), and exploring our solar system, among many other functions.

The main goal of the satellite (SLV-3) project was to launch a 40 kg satellite into orbit around the earth, 400 km above the earth's surface. It was a big challenge—Kalam needed all the help he could get. He asked for 275 engineers and scientists for the project, but received only fifty.

Each member of the SLV-3 team was an expert in his own field. Much like all scientists, they were very smart and liked to work on their own. 'It would be a task to make them work together,' Kalam thought.

He realised that the best way was to develop a balance—sometimes be actively involved and 'hands-on' about the project but at other times, being 'hands-off' and let the members be. This would be the best way to motivate this group of great minds and make them work together.

This method worked really well. The SLV-3 team not only succeeded in their project, but many team members went on to become leaders in other important science and technology programmes in India. Kalam's leadership had helped them grow and prepare for even bigger challenges in the future.

Chapter Six

Kalam found himself terribly hard pressed for time after assuming the leadership of the SLV-3 project. As the manager, he had to oversee everything from meetings, reviews and updates. He also had to be informed about an extensive range of subjects.

His day would begin with a 2 km walk around his lodge. It was during this time that he mentally prepared a general schedule, highlighting the things he wanted to accomplish on that day.

Once in office, Kalam first cleaned his table.

During the next ten minutes, he would scan all the papers, dividing them according to priority.

The SLV-3 design had over a million parts and it would take around seven to ten years to create. Thus, a project strategy was a must. Prof. Dhawan decided that all funds and manpower at VSSC and SHAR would be directed to Kalam's team.

Kalam's team developed different and innovative techniques to build the SLV-3. They also decided to build important machines in-house, like the huge 254-litre vertical mixer.

However, many of the SLV-3's parts were so massive, complex, and expensive that industries in the private sector had to be approached for funding. It also needed complicated electrical circuitry—all the electrical systems together is known as 'Avionics'.

The team also developed a variety of special tools to measure things like pressure, thrust, vibration, and acceleration. A special system was also made to destroy the rocket in case it malfunctioned. Solid fuel was chosen to make the rocket fly.

Kalam and his team faced many problems on a regular basis. But, they never gave up.

Meanwhile, the Defence Research and Development Organisation (DRDO) was working towards developing a surface-to-air missile, with Narayanan leading the team. Narayanan's team studied a Russian missile called the SA-2 to learn how to make their own. The missile project was code named 'Devil' and in February 1972, a funding of about Rs 5 crore was sanctioned for it for the first three years.

A surface-to-air missile, also known as SAM, is a missile launched from the ground, tank, or ship to destroy other missiles and aircraft. It is a type of anti-aircraft warfare.

Nazi Germany was the first country to develop surface-to-air missiles during the Second World War, but none of them reached working status as the war ended before that.

The Nike Ajax (official name MIM-3/3A) was the first official SAM system. It was activated by the USA in March 1954.

Nike Hercules was the first nuclear-tipped SAM.

India's Akash SAM system can engage multiple targets simultaneously and serves both the Indian Army and the Indian Air Force.

Narayanan was promoted to Air Commodore, and took over as Director, Defence Research and Development Laboratory (DRDL). He was an extremely energetic man and created a team of enthusiasts, recruiting many service officers.

At VSSC, the SLV project proceeded slowly, while the DRDL was racing ahead. But Kalam knew that patience was the key to the SLV's success. He wrote in his diary:

> *'If you want to leave your footprints on the sands of Time,*
> *Do not drag your feet.'*

Prof. Dhawan proved to be an able commander of the ISRO ship. He introduced the system to review the progress of the entire team involved in the project so that the work progressed smoothly.

In 1975, ISRO was declared a government body and the ISRO council was formed with Directors from various centres and senior officers from the Department of Space (DOS). TN Seshan, the Joint Secretary in the DOS was invited to participate in a SLV-3 Management Board meeting. Viewing Seshan as a typical bureaucrat, Kalam wasn't too happy about his involvement. But meeting the Joint Secretary changed his perception. He was extremely professional, had an analytical mind and had come prepared for the meeting. And this was enough to impress Kalam.

Chapter Seven

Deadlines were set to complete the SVL-3 smoothly. Kalam and his team planned to test the rocket parts by 1975, do short flights by 1976, and finally launch the satellite in 1978. It was an exciting time for India and on 24 July 1974, Prime Minister Indira Gandhi addressed the Parliament to announce the launch scheduled in 1978.

But hard days were approaching Kalam. One day, he received the news that his brother-in-law and one of his closest friends, Ahmed Jallaluddin had passed away. Kalam was numb with shock, and realised a part of him had died too. He recalled the evening walks with Jallaluddin in Rameswaram, both of them watching the sunset together. Jallaluddin was like an older brother to him, arranging money for Kalam's books and helping him out any way possible when he was young.

It was a tragedy. More for Kalam's father, who was more than a hundred years old, and had to be the pallbearer for his son-in-law. Kalam's sister Zohara too was heartbroken, having not healed from the wounds of losing her four-year-old son, she had now lost her husband.

Kalam reached Rameswaram the next day. They laid Jallaluddin's body to rest. Death had never frightened Kalam before, but Jallaluddin's death came as a shock; the man had gone too soon. Kalam could not stay at home for long. As his mother blessed him in a choked voice, he had a sad realisation. 'Have I been too busy to ignore my own family?' Kalam thought, consumed by guilt.

In 1976, Kalam lost his father. The great man had been 102 years old and had left behind fifteen grandchildren and one great-grandson. Soon after, his mother passed away too. In the same mosque that his father had taken him all his childhood, Kalam mourned his parents.

Racked with grief and guilt, he asked Allah for forgiveness.

'Why do you mourn their day of accomplishment? Concentrate on the work that lies before you, and proclaim My glory through your deeds,' someone seemed to encourage him.

Kalam exited the mosque, his mind at peace. He went back to Thumba the next morning, physically and emotionally drained, but determined to fulfil his dream of flying an Indian rocket on foreign soil.

Over the next few months, things began to look up for Kalam. After a successful testing of the SVL-3 motor in France, he returned to hear that the famous rocket scientist, the legendary Wernher von Braun—the man who had helped America send the first man to the moon—was to arrive in India.

Kalam received von Braun at Madras and then escorted him to Thumba. During their flight, the rocket scientist asked Kalam about his work, and listened as if he was a student of rocketry. Kalam was amazed that the father of modern rocketry could be so humble, responsive, and encouraging.

As he observed the progress of the SLV-3, von Braun gave Kalam sound advice: 'If you want to do anything in rocketry, do it yourself,' he said. 'The SLV-3 is a genuine Indian design, and you might be having your own troubles. But we don't just build on successes, but also on failures.'

'Hard work is not enough in rocketry,' von Braun told Kalam. 'You must have a goal and strategies in place to achieve it quickly. Total commitment is not just hard work, but total involvement. Building a rock wall is back-breaking work, and some people build rock walls throughout their lives. But, some have a vision or a goal in mind as they build a rock wall to create a terrace or enclose an orchard. They have more than a wall when they finish. It's the goal that makes the difference. Don't make rocketry your profession. Make it your religion, your mission in life.'

> The Saturn V was used in the Apollo program in the 1960s and 1970s, and was also used to launch Skylab, the first American space station.
>
> Flown from 1967 to 1973, the Saturn V rocket was used for nine crewed flights to the Moon.
>
> The rocket was 363 feet tall, the height of a thirty-six-storey building, and 60 feet taller than the Statue of Liberty.
>
> As of 2024, the Saturn V remains the only launch vehicle to have carried humans beyond the low Earth orbit (LEO).

Kalam thought he saw something of Dr Vikram Sarabhai in Wernher von Braun.

With three deaths in as many successive years, Kalam truly needed total commitment to keep working. He threw all his weight behind the SLV-3 project, as if it was his sole purpose in life. He even sacrificed his special badminton time during the evening, and weekends, holidays, and time with family and friends.

One day in 1979, a six-member team was working on a tank full of dangerous, red, fuming nitric acid when the tank burst. All the team members suffered severe acid burns. Even though they were hurt, the team was more worried about the project than their injuries.

Despite such hindrances, the SLV-3 project was finally completed in 1979. The first experimental flight trial took off; the first stage was performed to perfection. But, things went out of control in the second stage, and the flight had to be terminated after just 317 seconds. The vehicle's remains crashed into the sea.

Kalam and his team were devastated. Kalam was so exhausted physically and mentally that he went straight to his room and fell asleep. He decided a refreshed mind would better handle the crisis.

Later that day, a gentle touch to his shoulder woke him up. Dr Brahm Prakash was sitting by his bedside and asked him out for lunch. Kalam found out that he had come to his room twice before that, but had left after finding Kalam asleep. Kalam was touched by his concern and love.

Chapter Eight

On 11 August 1979, a post-flight review of the SLV-3 was attended by more than seventy scientists and a detailed research on the failure of the satellite launch was conducted. They reached the conclusion that since the second stage control system had failed, the vehicle became unstable and crashed into the sea. Further investigation showed that it was because of a leak in the fuel tank that had resulted in the second stage malfunction and failure.

Not someone to abandon his team during times of crisis, Kalam exhibited the attributes of a great leader. He stood up to Prof. Dhawan and said, 'Sir, I take the responsibility for judging the leak as insignificant. As the Mission Director, I should have put the launch on hold and saved the flight. I take full responsibility for the SLV-3 failure.'

There was pin-drop silence in the hall. Then, Prof. Dhawan rose, and declared, 'I'm going to put Kalam in orbit.'

The second SLV-3 was launched on 18 July 1980. After the first launch, it didn't seem like the country had much faith in its success. Thirty hours before the launch, the newspapers had started reporting about the previous failed launch and speculations about how the Project Director was missing and could not be contacted. Despite these negative thoughts, Kalam felt the launch would go perfectly—it had to! It would be instrumental in deciding the future of India's space programme.

At 8.03 a.m. on 18 July, India's first Satellite Launch Vehicle, SLV-3, lifted off from SHAR. Within the next two minutes, Rohini was set into a low earth orbit. In the midst of cheers, Kalam spoke the most important words in his life, 'Mission Director calling all stations. Stand by for an important announcement. All stages performed to mission requirements. The fourth stage apogee motor has given the required velocity to put Rohini Satellite into orbit.'

Kalam was lifted onto the shoulders of his jubilant colleagues, and carried in a procession. Every Indian was excited as India had entered a small group of nations that possessed satellite launch capability. The event was in newspaper headlines, and on special programmes aired by the radio and television stations. The Parliament greeted the achievement by thumping desks. It was the culmination of a national dream and the beginning of an important phase in India's history.

Prime Minister Indira Gandhi cabled her congratulations. But, to Kalam, the most precious reaction was that of the Indian scientific community who were proud of his effort.

Kalam was happy but at the back of his mind, he missed his inspirations—his father and Dr Sarabhai—who unfortunately couldn't witness this milestone in his career.

Within a month of the SLV-3's success, Kalam was invited to the Nehru Science Centre in Bombay to share his experiences. He received a telephone call soon after from Prof. Dhawan asking Kalam to join him in Delhi to meet the Prime Minister.

Never one for extravagance, Kalam usually dressed in casual clothes and slippers.

'How do I meet the Prime Minister like this? But I do not own anything fancy enough to meet the Prime Minister!' he asked Prof. Dhawan.

'Don't worry,' he assured Kalam. 'You are beautifully clothed in your success.'

At the Parliament House the next morning, Kalam met the Prime Minister, Indira Gandhi and thirty members of the Lok Sabha and Rajya Sabha.

'Kalam! We would like to hear you speak,' a smiling Indira Gandhi requested.

Standing in front of some of the most important personalities of the country, Abdul Kalam hesitantly said, 'I am honoured to be in this great gathering of nation-builders. I only know how to build a rocket system which would inject a satellite built in our country, by imparting to it a velocity of 25,000 km per hour.'

He was greeted by thunderous applause.

With Project SVL-3 a success, Kalam moved on to become the Director, Aerospace Dynamics and Design Group. He was ready to develop many more such launch vehicles for India.

The next SLV-3 flight, the SLV3-D1, took off on 31 May 1981, but Kalam had to watch the launch from the visitor's gallery. It made him sad that though he had helped create the first launch vehicle, since he was no longer part of the team, he wasn't allowed in the Control Centre anymore. But he quickly steeled himself, proud that his colleagues were taking him dream forward!

The year 1981 began with exciting news for Kalam. In January, in a chance encounter with famous nuclear scientist, Professor Raja Ramanna in Dehradun, Kalam was offered a position at the DRDL for their Guided Missile Development Programme (GMDP).

But the most exciting news came on 25 January! The next day, on the thirty-first Republic Day of India, Abdul Kalam would be conferred the prestigious Padma Bhushan Award.

'I feel as if my son has got the award,' Dr Brahm Prakash said when he called to congratulate.

Kalam celebrated quietly by playing Bismillah Khan's shehnai in his room. The music transported him back to the Rameswaram of his childhood. He was hugging his mother as his father caressed his hair lovingly. Jallaluddin had announced the news and a crowd had gathered on Mosque Street. His sister, Zohara served special sweets. Pandit Lakshmana Sastry applied a tilak on Kalam's forehead as his teacher Reverend Solomon blessed him. Kalam thought he also saw Dr Sarabhai smiling proudly.

Chapter Nine

Kalam's Padma Bhushan received mixed reactions at VSSC. Some shared his happiness, while others, including some of his closest colleagues, were jealous because he was singled out for recognition. Kalam realised that a time for change had come after eighteen long years spent at ISRO. With this in mind, he accepted Raja Ramanna's offer to join the DRDL.

But ISRO wasn't ready to let go of their star scientist! After many letters were exchanged and many meetings were conducted, Kalam was finally appointed as Director, DRDL in February 1982. Prof. Ramanna had retired and was replaced by Dr Arunachalam as the Scientific Advisor to the Defence Minister, R Venkataraman.

Narayanan's Devil missile project had also been shelved by the Ministry of Defence by then. All the young scientists who had worked hard on it were very disappointed. They felt cheated. So, when Admiral Dawson, the Chief of Naval Staff, visited DRDL, Kalam decided that the best way to cheer his new colleagues and inspire them would be to raise hope once again. He used the occasion of the Admiral's visit to make a point with his team. Many of the DRDL's projects were incomplete, one of them being the Tactical Core Vehicle (TCV) Project. To pique the Admiral's interest, Kalam emphasised on the TVC's ability to skim the ocean surface and how it would benefit the Navy.

This demonstration had an underlying message for his team: 'Don't make anything you can't sell later. Missile development is a multidimensional business and one couldn't afford to get stuck in one dimension.'

Kalam was impressed by the dedicated DRDL workforce, and invited experts from various educational institutions to interact with them and offer a fresh perspective. All of them together formed the Missile Technology Committee.

It was decided that the Guided Missile Development Programme would develop and produce two missiles. Kalam made a presentation to the Defence Minister R Venkataraman and other chiefs and ministers from the defence ministry. Everyone had doubts about the project—the team's capability, and the cost and time needed to complete it. Despite that, they were still hopeful and excited about this new avenue in India's defence system.

After Kalam's passionate pitch, the Defence Minister asked them to meet him three hours later. Kalam knew that his pitch had gone well and thought there would be some progress, but to his surprise, the Defence Minister gave the green light to launch the project.

That night, Dr Arunachalam and Kalam re-worked and finalised their plan. A set of four missiles were conceptualised—Prithvi, which could be launched from the ground; Trishul, a quick-reaction missile; Akash, to defend against attacks from the air; Nag, designed to stop tanks; and finally Agni, a family of long-range missiles.

As Kalam got ready to present this updated plan to the Defence Minister, he had a sudden disappointing realisation! Today was his niece, Zameela's wedding!

'How could I have forgotten about it? What shall I do now? There is no way to reach Rameswaram on time,' he thought, feeling dejected.

Kalam felt a pang of guilt and sadness wash over him. Zameela was like a daughter to him, and the thought of missing her special day weighed heavily on his heart. Yet, he knew the importance of his work for the nation. This internal conflict between personal commitments and professional duty would become a recurring theme in his life.

A guilty Kalam presented the new missile programme blueprint to the Defence Minister. Luckily, the Defence Minister was very impressed and cleared the project immediately. Kalam was delighted, but he still felt guilty about missing the wedding.

'Why do you look so dejected Kalam? Smile, the project is approved!' the minister asked.

'Yes sir, I am happy...'

'Actually sir, he is missing his niece's wedding. It is in the evening at Rameswaram and the poor man is stuck here with us,' Dr Arunachalam interjected.

'Is that so? That is unfortunate. Let me see

what we can do...Kalam, how do you feel about riding in an Air Force helicopter?' the Defence Minister asked with a smile.

Kalam was truly overwhelmed. Thanks to the generosity of the Defence Minister, he travelled to Madurai in an Air Force helicopter and reached home just in time to bless his brother's daughter with a father's love.

India's Guided Missile Development Programme (IGMDP) was passed by the Cabinet and Rs 388 crores was sanctioned to fund the project. On 27 July 1983, the IGMDP was formally launched at the DRDL. Every single employee of the DRDL was present as were several scientists from other organisations, professors from academic institutions, representatives from the armed forces, and DRDL's business partners. It was the second-most significant day in Kalam's career, after the SLV-3 launch.

A guided missile is controlled throughout its motion and can be guided into contact with a moving target. As the target changes its direction, the path of the missile can be changed accordingly.

Missiles can carry explosives or other loads and these are called the 'payload' of a missile. This payload is not always harmful to people.

A key name in India's Integrated Guided Missile Development Program was Tessy Thomas, also known as the 'Missile Woman' of India. Her work contributed greatly to India's missile technology.

Chapter Ten

With the project approved and funds gathered, the real challenge was to become experts in missile technology. Help from outside India was ruled out—they needed to do it at home and on their own! Kalam knew he needed leaders who would put their heart and soul into the missile programme. He reorganised the laboratory to work better and chose five special people to lead each missile project: Colonel VJ Sundaram to lead the Prithvi project, Commodore SR Mohan, an ex-Indian Navy man for Trishul, RN Agarwal for Agni, and young Prahlada and NR Iyer for Akash and Nag. At the very first Council meeting, a senior scientist, MN Rao, asked cheekily, 'On what basis did you select these five Pandavas?'

'Wait and watch,' Kalam told Rao. 'Every day will give opportunities to these five enthusiastic people to gain a fresh perspective of their goals and a strong hold on their commitments.'

The questions didn't stop. 'How are you going to stop these projects from going the Devil way?' someone else asked.

'There is no going back!' Kalam said. 'Now that we have begun, we will not stop till all the missiles are deployed.'

As the project began, Kalam realised they needed more space to work. The nearby area of Imarat Kancha looked perfect for this and

Kalam decided to build a research centre there. The Military Engineering Services asked for five years to complete the task, but since the project was on priority, the Ministry of Defence entrusted an outside construction company to finish the job quickly.

Chandipur in the Balasore district of Orissa was chosen as the site for the missile flight trials. But technology should never harm or come in the way of nature so Kalam asked his engineers to be extra careful and design the test range without disturbing the beautiful bird sanctuary there.

In September 1983, Defence Minister R Venkataraman visited DRDL to check on the missile progress.

'What you imagine, is what will transpire,' he declared. 'What you believe, is what you will achieve.'

The next year, Kalam and his team made an important breakthrough. They had created a guidance system for the project but they needed a missile to test it.

'I wonder if we can use the discontinued Devil for this...' Kalam thought.

The Devil was modified and a make-shift launcher was created. On 26 June 1984, the Devil was launched to test the new guidance system.

To everyone's delight, the system worked perfectly.

Word reached Delhi, and Prime Minister Indira Gandhi decided to personally congratulate the team on the progress of IGMDP, and visited the facility on 19 July 1984.

'When are you going to test flight Prithvi?' she asked Kalam.

'June 1987,' he replied.

'Let me know what's needed to accelerate the flight schedule,' she stated.

Within a month of her visit, Indira Gandhi sent the new Defence Minister, SB Chavan for review. With him came one of Kalam's old acquaintances, TN Seshan. Seshan was funny, loud and argumentative most of the time. But when it came to work, he was always the one who asked pointed questions and was able to make the best use of resources. Kalam was happy to have him on board.

The two had a funny relationship! Seshan was

also the only person who liked to use Kalam's full name every time he addressed him. And it was really long with thirty-one letters—Avul Pakir Jainulabdeen Abdul Kalam!

On 31 October 1984, the news of Prime Minister Indira Gandhi's assassination reached Kalam's ears. He and his team were preparing an action plan from the review to show to the Prime Minister at that time, and it saddened Kalam to hear of the loss of such a respected leader and supporter of the scientific community. Her son, Rajiv Gandhi became India's new Prime Minister and luckily was happy to carry forward her legacy. IGMDP still had the green light!

Indira Gandhi was the first woman Prime Minister of India and was known as the 'Iron Lady of India', being the most powerful woman in the world during her tenure.

On 31 October 1984, Indira Gandhi was assassinated by two of her Sikh bodyguards, seeking retribution for the humiliation of Sikhs by the Indian Army's 'Operation Blue Star' at the holy Golden Temple from where terrorists were flushed out.

The popular leader's assassination sent shockwaves through the country, unleashing some of the worst, shocking, and vicious communal violence ever witnessed.

In just three days, approximately 3350 Sikhs were killed, according to government estimates, 2800 in the national capital, New Delhi alone.

Prime Minister Rajiv Gandhi laid the foundation stone of Research Centre Imarat (RCI) at Imarat Kancha on 3 August 1985. Kalam liked his childlike curiosity, and he also possessed his mother's grit and determination. Addressing the DRDL family, the Prime Minister said he was aware of their hardships, and thanked the scientists who had chosen to work in their motherland rather than seek lucrative employment abroad. He assured them that their lives would be made more comfortable.

Chapter Eleven

Two hundred and eighty young engineers worked at the DRDL under Kalam's guidance. They created a productive work culture—both young and experienced scientists worked together towards a common goal—creating missiles for India!

On 16 September 1985, the first launch of the Missile Programme was conducted. Trishul took off successfully from a test range. This was followed by the successful test flight of the Pilotless Target Aircraft. Various academic institutions such as the Indian Institute of Science (IISc), Bangalore and Jadavpur University, Kolkata helped develop important software and guidance systems for the missiles.

Soon after, on a bright morning on 25 February 1988, at exactly 11.23 a.m., the missile Prithivi was launched. Prithvi could carry a 1000 kg warhead up to 150 km with great accuracy. It was so versatile that it could be used from land, air, or sea. The launch of Prithvi by India sent shock waves across the unfriendly neighbouring countries. Some were angry and tried to stop India from buying technology that was remotely missile-related. But this only made India more determined to become self-reliant.

India became a part of the select club of nations that were deemed superpowers. More than a show of might, Kalam considered it India's self-reliance in the world of advanced technology.

Agni was to be launched next, a missile on which more than five hundred scientists had worked on.

On 20 April 1989, the entire nation watched with bated breath.

But something malfunctioned right before they could hit the launch button. The computer signalled 'Hold' indicating that one of the instruments wasn't functioning properly. To everyone's horror, soon, multiple 'Holds' lit up the various computer screens. The launch had to be aborted.

Kalam knew he needed to keep the morale high.

'Your missile is right in front of you,' he

declared. 'You have lost nothing but time. All you need is a few weeks of rework.'

Kalam's team tried again on 1 May 1989. But another malfunction cropped up and the launch was postponed once more. In rocket science, such failures are common. But the nation was expecting great things, and was too impatient to comprehend the difficulties of a launch of this magnitude. A cartoon portrayed Agni as 'IDBM—Intermittently Delayed Ballistic Missile.' Amul's cartoon suggested Agni use their butter as fuel!

With each joke and cartoon, the team's disappointment increased.

'Maybe Agni would never be launched...' they wondered. Kalam had to do something!

On 8 May, Kalam decided to address the DRDL-RCI community of 2000 people.

'A great opportunity has been given to us to develop a missile system like Agni,' he said. 'Major opportunities come with major challenges, and we should not let this problem defeat us. The country deserves success from us, so let's aim for it. I promise you that we shall be together again after launching Agni successfully before the end of this month.'

Energised, the team worked non-stop to make the system ready in just ten days.

On 22 May 1989 they were ready to try again. Defence Minister KC Pant had come to witness the launch. The night before the launch, Kalam, Dr Arunachalam, and General KN Singh took a walk on the beach with the Defence Minister. It was a beautiful full-moon night and the waves were crashing on the shore. All of them were thinking the same thing. Will the Agni launch be successful tomorrow?

'Kalam, what would you like me to do to celebrate the Agni launch tomorrow?' the Defence Minister asked.

Kalam thought for a while and replied, 'We need 100,000 saplings to plant at RCI.'

'To buy the blessings of Mother Earth for

Agni,' KC Pant smiled and stated. 'We will succeed tomorrow!' he declared.

Agni took off at 7.10 a.m. the next day. It was a perfect launch. Six hundred seconds of elegant flight instantly washed away the endless fatigue of the entire team.

'The country is proud of your efforts,' Prime Minister Rajiv Gandhi said to Kalam.

'It's a tribute to your dedication, hard work, and talent,' President Venkataraman said to Kalam.

The world was in a tizzy! USA was far from pleased with India's success. The *Wall Street Journal* made the claim that India had made Agni with Germany's help. Germany denied this, and wondered if France offered help instead. Back in India, APJ Abdul Kalam had a good laugh. 'It is only the beginning,' he thought with a smile.

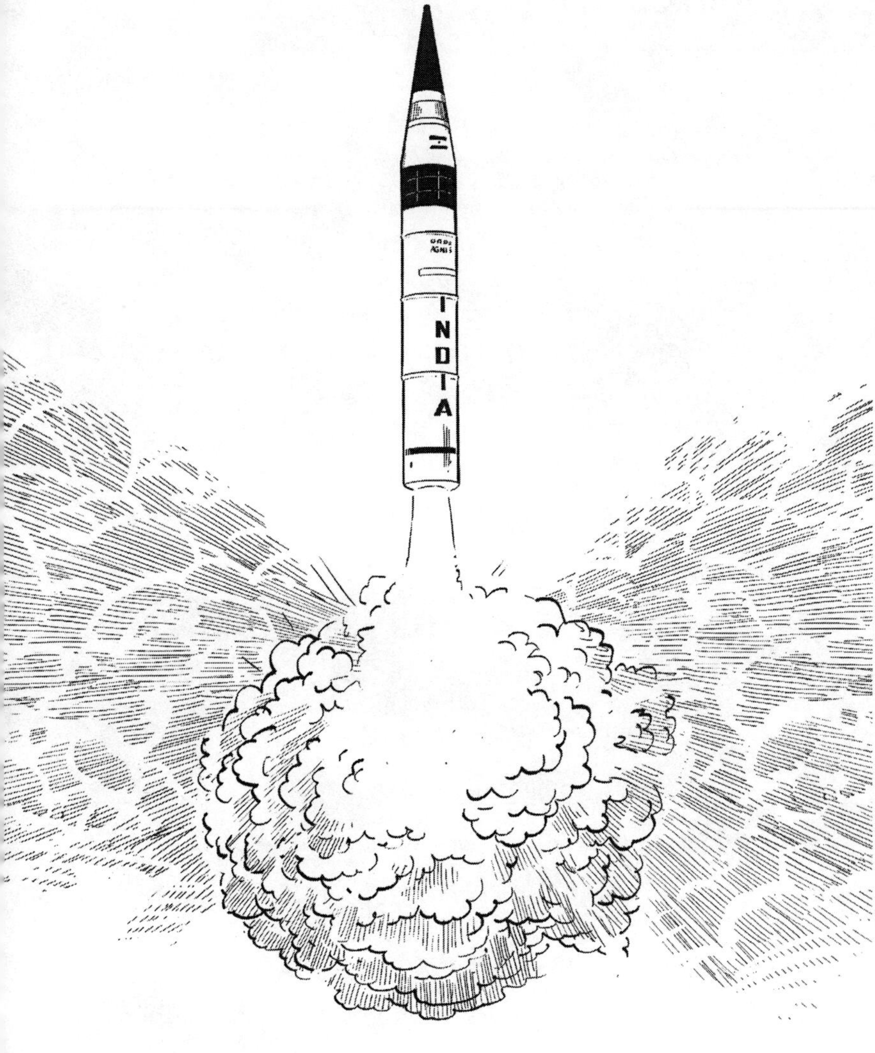
AGNI 5
INDIA

'India's indigenous technological advancement will lead to further glory.'

Agni-V, India's first ICBM or Inter-Continental Ballistic Missile was successfully test-fired in 2012. With a range of 5000 km, it cannot be stopped once fired.

Travelling faster than a bullet, Agni-V can carry 1000 kilograms of nuclear weapons, and can be launched even from a roadside. But the missile can only be launched with an approval from the Cabinet Committee on Security (CCS).

The three stages of the missile are powered by solid propellants. The first rocket engine takes it to a height of 40 km above the Earth, the second stage to a height of 150 km, and the third stage to about 300 km. Finally, the missile reaches a height of 800 km.

Agni-V can be configured to launch small satellites and also to shoot down enemy satellites in orbits.

Chapter Twelve

India finally celebrated the missile programme on Republic Day, 1990. At the same time, Abdul Kalam received the Padma Vibhushan Award along with Dr Arunachalam. That's not all! Two of Kalam's colleagues, RN Agarwal and JC Bhattacharya also received the Padma Shree Awards. For the first time in India's history, so many scientists affiliated to the same organisation found their names on the awards list.

At breakfast, as Kalam sat eating his idli and buttermilk, a mess bearer came and congratulated him for the award. Kalam was touched. 'No money is worth the love I have received from the country! I feel so lucky,' he thought.

As Kalam held the prestigious award, he reflected on his journey from the small island of Rameswaram to the national stage. He realised

that his success was not just his own, but a testament to India's potential. 'This award,' he thought, 'is a responsibility to continue pushing the boundaries of what our nation can achieve.'

Soon after, Kalam was invited to the Madurai Kamaraj University to deliver their convocation address. But after reaching Madurai, the first thing he did was locate his old high school teacher Reverend Iyadurai Solomon. He was one of the first people outside Kalam's family who truly believed in him.

The student and teacher had an emotional reunion and Kalam even brought Reverend Solomon to the convocation.

After a successful lecture, when Kalam bowed before his eighty-year-old teacher, he said, 'Kalam, you have not only achieved my goals, but eclipsed them.' The Reverend's voice was choked with emotion.

That same year, on India's forty-fourth Independence Day, Kalam and his team celebrated by test-firing Akash. Later that year, Kolkata's Jadavpur University conferred the prestigious honour of Doctor of Science on Kalam.

To all present at the convocation, Kalam only said this: 'Be more dedicated to making solid achievements than running after swift but synthetic happiness.'

The year 1990 was surely an exciting year, but 1991 began ominously, as the Gulf War broke out between Iraq and the US. Thanks to the television telecast of war images, rockets and missiles captivated the imagination of all Indians. Everyone was talking about them—in local tea shops and coffee houses. Even children had started playing with paper missiles.

THE GULF WAR TIMELINE

2 August 1990: Iraq invades Kuwait, a small, oil-rich nation. The decision was taken by Iraqi leader Saddam Hussein to pay off the debts incurred during Iraq's eight-year-war with Iran.

2 August 1990: The United Nations Security Council (UNSC) passes a resolution criticising the invasion.

6. August 1990: The UNSC imposes trade and financial sanctions on Iraq to stop her from trading with other countries.

7 August 1990: US President George Bush orders the beginning of Operation Desert Shield.

8 August 1990: Iraq announces the annexation of Kuwait, which is declared illegal by the UNSC.

29 November 1990: The UNSC authorises the use of force after 15 January 1991.

16-17 January 1991: The air campaign, Operation Desert Storm, begins.

23-24 February 1991: An Allied ground assault begins with a forty-two countries, led by the United States.

27 February 1991: Baghdad radio announces that Iraq will comply with UN resolutions.
Kuwait is liberated.

28 February 1991: Attacks against Iraq come to a stop.

14 March 1991: Kuwait's Emir returns home after more than seven months in exile.

6 April 1991: Iraq accepts the terms of a ceasefire agreement.

The successful test firing of Prithvi and Trishul during the Gulf War made India feel secure. But Indians were always drawing parallels of the nation's indigenous missiles with missiles like Scud and Patriot that were operational in the Gulf War. Could Prithvi match up to a Scud? Would Akash perform like a Patriot?

Always optimistic, Kalam would say 'Yes' or 'Why not?' whenever he was asked these questions. But the truth was that the Allied forces had slightly better technology so their missiles were also of slightly superior quality. India was still catching up, but she wouldn't stay behind for too long.

After the Gulf War ended, more than 500 scientists from India's scientific community gathered to discuss the emerging issues.

'How can we make our missiles as great as those of the other countries?' Kalam asked some of the brightest minds in the country.

Ideas were thrown, arguments were had, and by the end, each and every scientist vowed that they would do their best to contribute to the betterment of India's missile system.

When Dr Kalam turned sixty and was ready to retire, he decided the best way to take his legacy forward would be to open a school for less privileged children. He hoped that the younger generation would produce equally bright minds enthusiastic about science and eager to help the nation prosper.

The Rao-Kalam school was planned in partnership with his friend Professor P Rama Rao, head of the Department of Science & Technology.

The two friends planned excitedly for this new venture, but destiny had other plans. Or rather, the Government of India was not ready to let go of the two gems, so their retirement was postponed, and in 1992, Kalam was appointed Chief Scientific Advisor to the Prime Minister.

But Kalam never forgot his love for teaching. And, in December 2001, he decided to follow his heart and started teaching at Anna University, Chennai. Little did Kalam know that his teaching career would only last eight months.

Chapter Thirteen

On 10 June 2002, as Kalam was returning to his room after the last lecture of the day, the Vice Chancellor of Anna University rushed to the seventy-year-old professor.

'Someone is desperately trying to reach you,' the Vice Chancellor informed. 'We have received several calls.'

Confused, Kalam reached his room to find the telephone ringing. He picked it up, and a voice on the other said, 'The Prime Minister wants to talk to you.'

While Kalam waited to be connected, his cellphone buzzed. It was the Chief Minister of Andhra Pradesh, Chandrababu Naidu.

'Expect an important call from the Prime Minister,' he said, adding, 'Please don't say no!'

'What is going on?' Kalam wondered.

Prime Minister Atal Bihari Vajpayee came straight to the point as the line was connected. 'We have some important news for you. I have just returned from a special meeting attended by the leaders of all the coalition parties. We have decided unanimously that the nation needs you as its President. I have to announce this tonight, and I need your consent. I need a "Yes", and not a "No".'

What an interesting turn of events! Kalam was intrigued, shocked, unsure, excited—he felt a range of emotions.

Asking the Prime Minister for a little time, he called his closest friends. For the next two hours, they worked on the pros and cons of such a decision.

The opinion was divided.

While some said, 'Why do you want to disturb your life now? You are at such a good place in your life. You love teaching, the students love you—there are more than triple the number of students in each class! You should stick to it.'

Others said, 'Of course, you should take it! This is a once-in-a-lifetime opportunity. You should not miss it.'

Kalam was conflicted at first but he realised that being the President of India would only help him bring the country to greater glory. 'It is for the best,' he thought.

Kalam let the Prime Minister know that he had agreed. The news travelled faster than a rocket, and within fifteen minutes, word spread across the country that Kalam was the choice as presidential candidate.

Although some were confused how a scientist could become the President of India, on 18 July 2002, Dr APJ Abdul Kalam was elected the 11th President of the Republic of India by a landslide victory.

Kalam served as President from 2002 to 2007, and was affectionately known as the 'People's President' because he was friendly, approachable, humble and wise. He was an inspirational leader and had some remarkable achievements during his presidential tenure.

- He devised a twenty-year action plan to achieve economic growth through technological development.
- He increased access to education and technology for all Indians.
- He established India as a leading player on the global stage.

The little boy from Rameswaram who worked as a newspaper vendor to earn some extra money had certainly come a long way. His dream was to fly, and fly he did!

On 27 July 2015, Dr APJ Abdul Kalam boarded his final flight. He passed away after suffering a cardiac arrest while delivering a lecture at IIM Shillong. Even in his last hours, the great man was working! The legacy of Abdul Kalam lives on, resonating in the heart of every Indian. He showed all of us that 'simple living and high thinking' was the key to achieving all of our dreams.

His poetic take on a verse by Edward Lear probably sums it up best:

'On the coast of Coromandel
Where the earthly shell blows
In the middle of the sands
Lived some really rich souls
One cotton lungi and half a candle
The old jug without a handle
These were all the worldly possessions
Of these kings in the middle of the sands.'

'If you want to shine like a sun, first burn like a sun.'

APJ ABDUL KALAM: A TIMELINE

- 15 October 1931: Avul Pakir Jainulabdeen Abdul Kalam is born in Rameswaram, Tamil Nadu, to Jainulabdeen Marakayar and Ashiamma.
- 1954: Kalam graduates in Physics from St Joseph's College, Tiruchirapalli.
- 1955: Kalam goes to Madras Institute of Technology (MIT) to study engineering.
- 1958: He joins the Aeronautical Development Establishment of the Defence Research and

Development Organisation (DRDO) as a scientist.

- 1960s: Kalam works on India's first Satellite Launch Vehicle programme.
- 1969: He is transferred to the Indian Space Research Organisation (ISRO) where he becomes project director of India's first satellite launch vehicle, the SLV-3.
- 1980s: Kalam plays a key role in developing the Polar Satellite Launch Vehicle. (PSLV).
- 1981: Kalam receives the Padma Bhushan award from the Government of India.
- 1990: He is honoured with the Padma Vibhushan award.
- 1992: Kalam is appointed the Chief Scientific Advisor to the Prime Minister of India.
- 1997: He is honoured with the Bharat Ratna.

- 1997-2002: Kalam is appointed and serves as the 11th President of India.
- 2002: He returns to his civilian life of writing, teaching, and public service.
- 2009: Kalam becomes the first Asian to be honoured with the Hoover medal, America's top engineering prize.
- 27 July 2015: Dr APJ Abdul Kalam passes away after a cardiac arrest while delivering a lecture at IIM, Shillong.

Author's Note

While working on this book, the famous phrase, 'This is not rocket science!' often came to mind. We tend to use this phrase for something we feel is possible to achieve. But thanks to APJ Abdul Kalam, rocket science no longer seems to be that unachievable towering mountain that could not be scaled.

I was also struck by the importance of keeping things simple and the art of humility despite great achievements, as illustrated by the great man. APJ Abdul Kalam's greatness in the field of rocketry and his achievements are legendary, but his humane qualities and humble demeanour were the most inspiring for me.

I mostly referred to books penned by Kalam himself to keep things simple—*Wings of Fire*, *Ignited Minds*, and *Learning How to Fly*. Along with that, archives of newspapers like the *Times of India*, *The Telegraph*, *The Hindu* and *The Deccan Herald* helped a lot with basic research.

I would like to thank Sudeshna Shome Ghosh for giving me the opportunity to pen down such an inspirational biography and Dyuti Roy for the wonderful edit. The illustrations by Mohit Suneja on the book have ornamented the content perfectly.

Thanks to my wife Piali Paul Ganguly, a member of the unofficial APJ Abdul Kalam Fan

Club, for the mammoth poster of Kalam she decided to put up in my study several years ago. It was rather comforting to see the great man smiling down upon me, approvingly I hope, as I worked on his biography. Hope you have as much fun reading this book as I had writing it.

Swayam Ganguly